W9-AMO-030

69

Kot

# A Day with a Doctor

## By Jan Kottke

Children's Press
A Division of Grolier Publishing
New York / London / Hong Kong / Sydney
Danbury, Connecticut

Photo Credits: Cover, all photos by Thaddeus Harden
Contributing Editor: Jennifer Ceaser
Book Design: Michael DeLisio

Visit Children's Press on the Internet at:
http://publishing.grolier.com

Cataloging-in-Publication Data

Kottke, Jan
    A day with a doctor / by Jan Kottke.
      p. cm — (Hard work)
    Includes bibliographical references and index.
    Summary: Explains in simple terms some of the work that
    doctors do.
    ISBN 0-516-23087-5 (lib. bdg.) — ISBN 0-516-23012-3 (pbk.)
    1. Physicians—Juvenile literature 2. Medicine—
Juvenile literature [1. Physicians 2. Occupations]
I. Title. II. Series.
    R690.K68 2000
    610.69'52—dc21

                                                    00-024388

# Contents

I take care of people who are sick.

I take care of people who are healthy.

I am a doctor.

5

I listen to your **chest**.

I can hear that your heart is healthy.

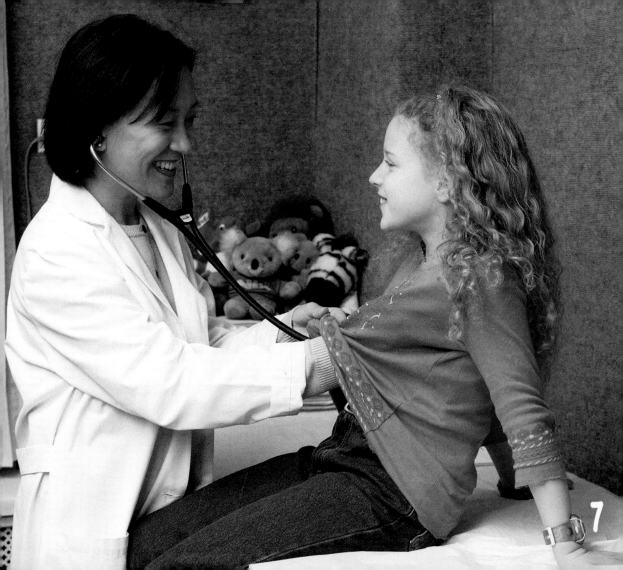

7

Open wide and say "Ah."

I check your throat and **tonsils**.

I make sure that they look healthy.

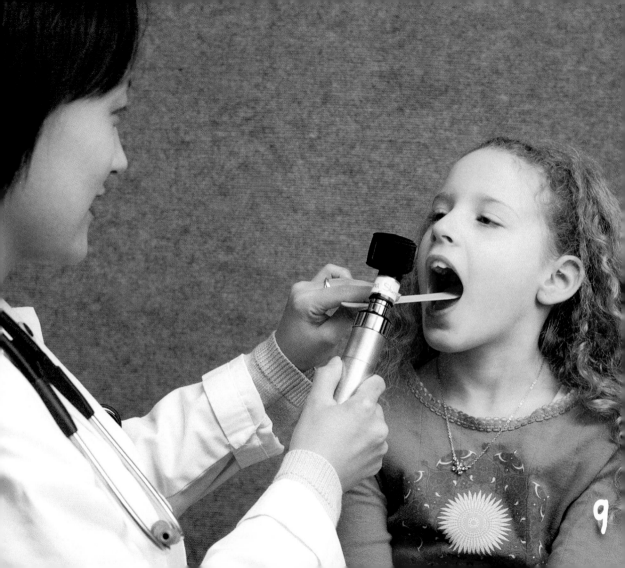

I look inside your ear with a light.

I check that your ear looks **normal**.

I make sure that you are growing.

I find out how tall you are.

I check how much you weigh.

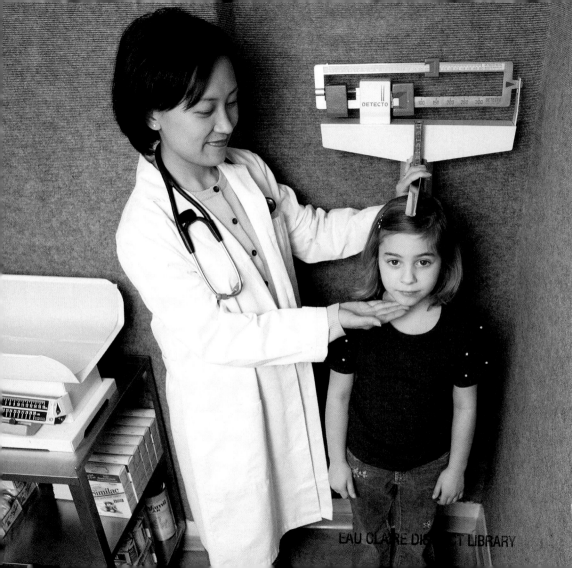

13

Are you not feeling well?

I need to **examine** you to see what is wrong.

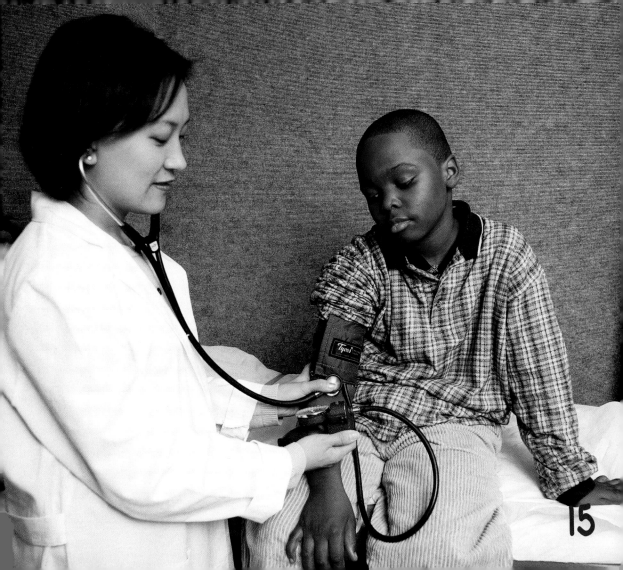

15

Does your head feel hot?

You have a **fever**.

This **medicine** will make your fever go away.

Sometimes you need to get a **shot**.

This shot will keep you healthy.

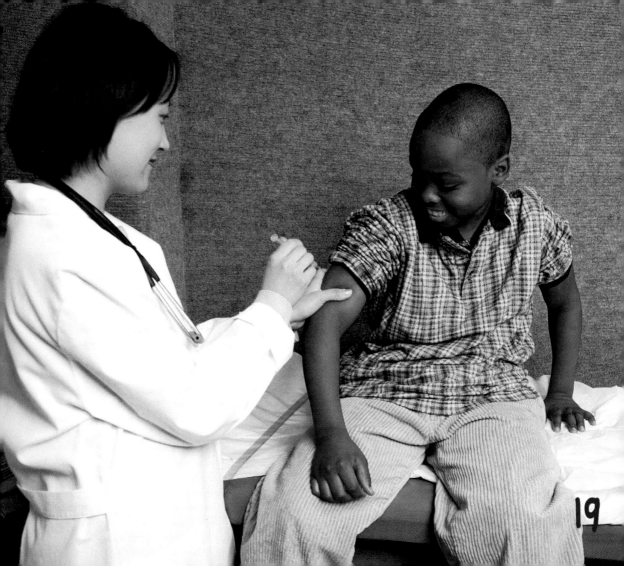
19

Everything is fine.

You are healthy.

I will see you for another **checkup** next year.

# New Words

**checkup** (**chek**-up) a visit where a doctor checks to see if you are healthy

**chest (chest)** the front of your body

**examine** (eg-**zam**-en) look at closely

**fever** (**fee**-ver) when your body feels warm because you are sick

**medicine** (**med**-e-sin) something given to treat you when you are sick

**normal** (**nor**-mul) healthy

**shot (shot)** medicine that is given with a needle

**tonsils** (**ton**-sulz) two small parts on the sides of your throat

# To Find Out More

**Books**
*Ask Nurse Pfaff, She'll Help You!*
by Alice K. Flanagan
Children's Press

*Doctors Help People*
by Amy Moses
The Children's World

*My Doctor, My Friend*
by P.K. Hallinan
Hambleton-Hill Publishing

**Web Site**
**Doctor Over Time**
http://www.pbs.org/wgbh/aso/tryit/doctor/#
Try the Doctor Over Time Activity to learn more about the history of doctors.

# Index

**About the Author**
Jan Kottke is the owner/director of several preschools in the Tidewater area of Virginia. A lifelong early education professional, she is completing a phonics reading series for preschoolers.

**Reading Consultants**
Shelly Forys, Certified Reading Recovery Specialist, W.J. Zahnow Elementary School, Waterloo, IL

Peggy McNamara, Professor, Bank Street College of Education, Reading and Literacy Program